Contents

Ash

bud

leaf

4

LEARNING ABOUT
Trees

Catherine Veitch

The author would like to dedicate this book to her mother, Jacqueline Veitch, who inspired her with a love of nature.

Raintree is an imprint of Capstone Global Library Limited, a company incorporated in England and Wales having its registered office at 7 Pilgrim Street, London, EC4V 6LB – Registered company number: 6695582

To contact Raintree:
Phone: 0845 6044371
Fax: + 44 (0) 1865 312263
Email: myorders@raintreepublishers.co.uk
Outside the UK please telephone +44 1865 312262.

Edited by Dan Nunn, Rebecca Rissman, and Sian Smith
Designed by Joanna Hinton-Malivoire
Picture research by Mica Brancic
Production by Sophia Argyris
Originated by Capstone Global Library Ltd
Printed and bound in China by South China Printing Company Ltd

ISBN 978 1 406 26609 2
17 16 15 14 13
10 9 8 7 6 5 4 3 2 1

British Library Cataloguing in Publication Data
A catalogue record for this book is available from the British Library.

Acknowledgements
We would like to thank Michael Bright for his invaluable help in the preparation of this book.

We would also like to thank the following for permission to reproduce photographs: Alamy pp.4 inset top (© Bob Gibbons), 8 main (© CuboImages srl/Paroli Galperti); FLPA pp.4 main (© Bob Gibbons), 5 inset bottom (Martin B Withers), 8 inset, 19 inset bottom (Marcus Webb), 16 main (Derek Hall), 19 inset top (Minden Pictures/© Adri Hoogendijk); Nature Picture Library pp.9 main (Mike Read), 16 inset bottom (© Simon Colmer); Photoshot pp.12 main (© NHPA/Kevin Schafer), 20 inset (© Cuboimages/Paroli Galperti), 20 main (© Photos Horticultural/Michael Warren), 23 flower (© Cuboimages/Paroli Galperti); Shutterstock pp.4 inset bottom (© Grigorii Pisotsckii), 4 inset top (© Ewa Studio), 5 main (© Chuck Cho), 6 (© Oleg Znamenskiy), 7 inset (© Tamara Kulikova), 7 main (© EastVillage Images), 9 inset (© marlee), 10 inset bottom (© Radka Palenikova), 10 inset top (© tolchik), 10 main (© Martina I. Meyer), 11 (© Maksym Gorpenyuk), 12 inset (© Julie Simpson), 13 inset (© William Berry), 13 main (© Zack Frank), 14 inset (© Nastya22), 14 main (© kosam), 15 inset (© Brandon Bourdages), 15 main (© Yusia), 16 inset top (© Sergej Razvodovskij), 17 inset (© Robyn Mackenzie), 17 main (© Konrad Weiss), 18 inset and main (© Alessandro Zocc), 19 main (© marilyn barbone), 21 inset (© Frank L Junior), 21 main (© Jeff Dalton), 22 bark (© EastVillage Images), 22 berry (© marlee), 22 blossom (© Ewa Studio), 22 branch (© marilyn barbone), 23 bud (© haraldmuc), 23 catkin (© Sergej Razvodovskij), 23 cone (© Alessandro Zocc), 23 fruit (© Brandon Bourdages), 23 leaf (© Radka Palenikova), 24 pine needles (© William Berry), 24 roots (© Maksym Gorpenyuk), 24 trunk (© EastVillage Images), 24 seeds (© Bobkeenan Photography).

Front cover photograph of a tree in autumn reproduced with permission of Shutterstock (© sonya etchison). Back cover photograph of a weeping willow tree reproduced with permission of Shutterstock (© Jeff Dalton).

Every effort has been made to contact copyright holders of material reproduced in this book. Any omissions will be rectified in subsequent printings if notice is given to the publisher.

Cherry

blossom

leaf

Dragon's blood

branch

trunk

Giant sequoia

bark

leaf

hazelnut

Holly

berry

leaf

Horse chestnut

seed

leaf

roots

Monkey puzzle

leaf

branch

North American pine

pine needles

Oak

acorn

leaf

Pear

fruit

trunk

Pussy willow

catkin

leaf

Silver birch

leaf

branch

trunk

17

Spruce

cone

seeds

leaf

19

Tulip tree

flower

catkin

Picture glossary

 **bark** rough, outer covering of a tree

 **berry** small, round fruit with one seed or lots of seeds inside

 **blossom** flowers that appear on a fruit tree before the fruit

 **branch** part of a tree that grows out of the tree's trunk. Branches help a tree to spread its leaves out.

 **bud** part of a plant that grows into a new leaf or a flower

22

 **catkin** small group of flowers on a short stem that grows on some trees

 **cone** hard case that keeps seeds safe. Fir and pine trees have seed cones.

 **flower** part of a plant that makes seeds. The smells flowers make and their colours help to attract insects.

 **fruit** fruits hold seeds. Plants make fruit so that animals will eat the fruit and carry the seeds to new places.

 **leaf** part of a plant. Leaves use sunlight to make food for the plant.

 **pine needles** long, thin, pointed leaves

 **roots** part of a plant that holds the plant in the ground. Roots bring water to the plant.

 **seeds** plants make seeds. Seeds grow into new plants.

 **trunk** main stem of a tree

Notes for parents and teachers

- Go on a nature walk with the children. Help them to identify different trees and their parts. Explain that trees are a type of plant. The children can sketch or photograph what they see. Use the pictures to make a class book.
- Collect different leaves and make some bark rubbings. Discuss the different shapes and colours of leaves, and the different bark patterns. Add the pressed leaves and bark rubbings to the class book. Remind children to always check with an adult that leaves are safe to collect, and to always wash their hands after handling leaves.

24